Connor Bedard

From Backyard Rinks to NHL

Dreams - A Kid's Biography

Daisy Katy

Copyright

All rights reserved. No part of this publication may be reproduced, distributed, or transmitted in any form or by any means, including photocopying, recording, and other electronic or mechanical methods, without prior written permission of the publisher, except in case of briefs quotation embodied in critical reviews and certain other noncommercial uses permitted by copyright law.

Copyright © Daisy Katy,2024

Table of Contents

Introduction   4

Chapter 1: Growing Up in British Columbia   12

Chapter 2: Becoming Exceptional: How Connor Got His "Exceptional Player" Status   21

    The Important Moment: Connor's Joy on Draft Day 30

Fun Facts About Connor Bedard   39

    Connor's Message to Young Athletes   45

Hockey Drills Inspired by Connor: Practice Like the Prodigy   50

    Q&A: Test Your Knowledge   63

Conclusion   72

Introduction

When it comes to hockey, Connor Bedard is one of the most exciting names. Connor was born on July 17, 2005, in North Vancouver, British Columbia. He played hockey all through school and was pretty much born with a stick in his hand. Kids in Canada, where hockey is the national sport, often skate on frozen ponds and wish they could be NHL stars. But it was clear that Connor was different from other kids even when he was very young.

Like a lot of other Canadian kids, Connor got into hockey through his family. He began skating when he was very young and spent hours on the ice with his friends shooting pucks and training. It was clear he loved the game, and he was always one of the kids who worked the hardest, staying on the rink longer than anyone else. But Connor wasn't just unique because of his passion; he was also incredibly talented. It was clear from his first games that he was good at what he did. Most kids his age couldn't skate or shoot as hard or think as fast as he did.

Connor's skills only got better as he aged. Scouts, coaches, and friends all saw that this young boy was different. He was much smarter than his years when it came to skating. He knew exactly where to pass the puck, when to shoot, and how to trick the other team. He was one of the most exciting young players to watch because he could score goals and make amazing plays. Connor wasn't just good; he was great.

Connor made hockey history when Hockey Canada gave him "exceptional status" when he was only 15 years old. People who are thought to be ready to play at a higher level younger than usual are the only ones who get this honor. This meant that Connor could join the Western Hockey League (WHL) even though he was younger than most of the other players. He was the first player in the league's history to get this position. Few other hockey stars, like Connor McDavid and John Tavares, were already famous in other leagues before they got to the NHL.

When Connor joined the Regina Pats of the WHL, he didn't just keep up with the other players; he crushed them. People who watched, coached, and even played with him were truly amazed by his skills. Not only was Connor playing against bigger, stronger, and more experienced players, but he was also beating them! People cheered when he scored goals, and his smarts on the ice made him a star player from the start. Though Connor was one of the league's youngest players, he played with the ease and skill of a much older player.

Connor's amazing journey doesn't end there, though. He also played for Canada in international games, and at the IIHF U18 World Championship, he helped his team win gold medals. People around the world saw that he was not only one of the best young players in Canada but also one of the best in the world. Every time Connor plays, he shows that he has what it takes to be a star, both in his own country and around the world.

A lot of people think that Connor is going to become the next big thing in hockey as he keeps getting better. He's already being compared to some of the best players ever, and NHL scouts are eagerly following his progress because they think he could be the first player picked in the next draft.

Connor Bedard is unique not only because of his skill but also because of how much he loves the game. Connor doesn't let all the attention and praise he gets distract him from what's important: getting better, working hard, and never losing sight of his goals. He works out longer and harder than everyone else, but he stays humble and always wants to do better.

One thing is clear about Connor Bedard's journey: he's already a hockey star, and he's only just getting started. A lot of good things are coming up for this young player. Every game he plays is another step toward becoming one of hockey's biggest stars. Fans all over the world are paying close attention because they know that Connor Bedard could be the future of the sport.

Chapter 1: Growing Up in British Columbia

For Connor Bedard, growing up in British Columbia meant being close to beautiful mountains and woods, as well as great weather for outdoor activities. Connor was born in North Vancouver on July 17, 2005. Hockey was more than just a game there; it was a way of life. Because it gets cold in Canada in the winter, ponds and outdoor rinks quickly became Connor's favorite place to play hockey. He was only a child the first time he went out on the ice, but he was hooked right away.

An awful lot of Canadian kids start skating almost as soon as they can walk. His parents took him to nearby rinks, where he and other kids would skate and chase pucks for hours. Connor had a lot of energy, even when he was young. He wasn't just skating for fun; he was working hard to improve his moves and dreamed of playing in the NHL like his hockey stars.

British Columbia was a great place for Connor to live because it has long winters and lots of outdoor activities. He was outside for a lot of the time, skating on frozen lakes or playing street hockey with his friends. Because it was cold and snowy, he felt like he was at home there. Connor loved hockey all the time, though, even when he wasn't outside. Inside, he would work on his stickhandling with a ball in any empty area he could find.

From the start, Connor's hard work was clear. Connor wasn't having fun while the other kids played hockey for fun. Putting in the time to get better was something he was willing to do. His folks saw early on how dedicated he was. He would practice his shots over and over, even when he was little because he was driven to get better each time. He wasn't happy with just being good; he wanted to be great.

Connor's early life in British Columbia shaped who he was and how he played the game. He had lots of room to play and explore because the area was so beautiful, but it also taught him important lessons about how to work hard and not give up. British Columbia has harsh winters with cold weather and a lot of snow, but Connor never let that stop him. He liked being cold and used every chance he had to work out and get stronger.

As Connor got bigger, he joined local hockey leagues and quickly moved up the ranks in the game. He was good at what he did, and soon he was competing with kids who were a lot older than him. Even though the other people were better, Connor never gave up. He wasn't as big as some of the other players, but his speed, skill, and drive made up for it. At first, he stood out because he could read the game and make smart moves.

Being able to play in British Columbia also gave Connor access to great coaches and training options. Many kids in the state want to play hockey in the NHL because it's such a big deal there. Connor did the same thing. He learned from his teachers and got better at the game every chance he got. Whether it was early practices or long drives to events, Connor's family helped him follow his dream and grow as a player.

In British Columbia, Connor's life was full of the kinds of exciting experiences that made him a well-rounded player. In his free time, he liked to play other sports, go climbing on the nearby beautiful trails, or spend time with his family. That's because all of these things helped him get stronger, more balanced, and more athletic, all of which would later become important parts of his ice game.

Connor's humility is one of the things that makes him stand out. Even though he was successful at first, he never let it get to him. Connor learned how important it is to stay humble, work hard, and always try to be better by growing up in British Columbia in a stable and loving home.

He played hockey not to show off, but because he loved it and wanted to be the best at it.

By the time Connor was a youth, his skill had taken him far beyond the rinks in his home province of British Columbia. Because he worked so hard, he was given special permission to join the Western Hockey League (WHL) when he was only 15 years old. He was the first player in WHL history to receive this honor. Many people around the world learned about Connor's ability and fame, but he stayed the same humble, hardworking kid from British Columbia.

It was in this beautiful part of Canada that Connor Bedard got the skills he needed to become one of the biggest stars in hockey. The snowy rinks and cold streets of British Columbia were where his love for the game, his drive to get better, and his willingness to work hard all began. Connor's trip isn't over yet, but the time he spent growing up in this special place will always be a big part of who he is.

Chapter 2: Becoming Exceptional: How Connor Got His "Exceptional Player" Status

Connor Bedard did something that not many hockey players ever do: Hockey Canada named him an "exceptional player." He was only 15 years old. He was able to join the Western Hockey League (WHL) a year before most players because of this rare honor. This showed that he was much smarter and more talented than his age. However, how did Connor become so special, and what does it mean to be given such an honorable title?

There was no doubt about it from a young age that Connor Bedard was not your average hockey player. It was clear that he was good at ice hockey, and his drive to work hard and his love for the game made him stand out from other kids his age. Connor always wanted to push himself harder and get better, while most young players just wanted to have fun and get better at a normal rate.

Connor was already making waves in the hockey world when he was 14. He played on teams in British Columbia, where he faced kids who were older and had more experience than him. But Connor did great instead of being scared. He beat most of the players he played against because he was faster, smarter, and more skilled. Scouts and teachers from all over the country quickly became interested in him. People took notice of how well he could read the game, make quick choices, and score goals. Not long after that, people began to call him a rising star.

Hockey Canada has only given this rank to a small group of young athletes. This title is given to players who are so skilled and developed that they can join big junior hockey leagues like the WHL, OHL, or QMJHL before they turn the normal age. This level of play means that players should be physically and mentally able to handle the pressures of playing with much older players. Connor Bedard was ready for the huge duty that came with it.

Before Connor, only a few players in other leagues had ever been named an "exceptional player." This was given to some of the biggest players in hockey, like John Tavares, Aaron Ekblad, and Connor McDavid, and all of them went on to have great careers in the NHL. When a player is given exceptional status, it means they can be truly special. Connor was about to join that small but elite group.

Hockey Canada didn't just look at Connor's on-ice skills when he applied to be a special player. They also looked at how mature he was, what kind of person he was, and how well he could handle the pressures that come with playing at such a high level. It's not enough to just be good at the game; you also have to be ready for the difficulties of playing against older, stronger, and more experienced people. Everyone was surprised by how calm and focused Connor was. He wasn't just physically ready for the next step; his mind was also ready.

Hockey Canada made it official in 2020: Connor Bedard was named an exceptional player. He was the first player in WHL history to receive this award. Connor could join the Regina Pats, one of the best teams in the WHL, at the age of 15. He would play against players who were sometimes five years older than him. Connor didn't let the pressure get to him, even though it was a big moment in his career. He saw it as a chance to keep getting better and show that he belonged at the top level.

Connor didn't just fit in with the Regina Pats team; he stood out. This player quickly became one of the best, even though he was one of the youngest in the game. He was lightning-fast, very skilled, and smart about hockey. He could play with and often beat guys who had been in the league for years. Connor scored goals and made plays that got fans and scouts excited in his first season. He didn't just have a title for being great; he earned it every time he stepped on the ice.

Connor didn't let the praise and attention get to him, though. People kept calling him names like some of the biggest names in hockey, but he stayed humble and worked hard to get better. Connor thought that being great wasn't just about being naturally skilled; it also meant working harder than everyone else and always wanting to get better. He studied the game, practiced his shot, and did skating drills for hours to make sure he was always ready for anything that came his way.

Connor's journey didn't start when he was named an "exceptional player." It meant that people saw how talented he was, but more than that, it made him work hard to meet the high standards that came with it. One thing Connor has shown is that he does well when things get tough. He shows everyone why he's one of the best young players in the game every time he steps on the ice.

No matter what Connor Bedard does in the WHL or elsewhere, his unique status will always be a defining moment in his life. This was the moment that proved he was more than just a good player; he was a unique talent that could alter the field. There is still a long way to go, but it's clear that Connor is ready to keep showing how great he is.

The Important Moment: Connor's Joy on Draft Day

*Being picked up by the NHL is the dream of every young hockey player. It's the moment when all the years of practice early in the morning and long hours on the ice truly pay off. Connor Bedard, on the other hand, was filled with joy, anticipation, and the achievement of a lifelong dream at that very moment.

It wasn't easy for Connor to get to the NHL draft. He was one of the most talked-about young hockey players. From his early years playing on rinks in British Columbia to becoming the first player in the history of the Western Hockey League (WHL) to be given "exceptional status," Connor's skill and hard work had hockey fans, scouts, and teams all over the world taking notice. When the draft came around, everyone knew that Connor would be one of the first picks.

But Connor stayed focused, even though things were getting exciting around him. That was the exact type of player he was: calm, controlled, and always ready for the next game. Before the draft, Connor kept playing very well. He dominated the WHL and showed everyone why he was thought to be a future NHL star. He stood out because of his strong shot, great skating, and smart hockey sense. As draft day got closer, it was clear that Connor was going to make history.

As a young hockey player, the NHL draft is one of the most exciting times in your life. Today is a day of feelings: worry, hope, and happiness. Because of Connor, today was the start of a new part of his trip. He had worked hard for years, and now he was about to find out which NHL team would pick him to be a part of their youth.

There was a lot of talk about Connor's future in the months before the draft. Hockey experts and researchers argued about which team would be lucky enough to pick him, and fans couldn't wait for Connor to join the NHL. And it was clear that whichever team got him would be getting a possible star player whose amazing skills could change the team's future.

Connor, his family, and himself were very excited on draft day. It was finally the day they had all been waiting for. This moment was the result of all the hours of hard work, commitment, and sacrifice. Connor could feel the excitement growing as he sat in the room with his family. As a child, he had thought of this moment while playing street hockey with his friends and making believe he was being picked up by the NHL. It was now real.

Connor waited calmly as the names of other players were called. He knew his turn would soon come. Then it was finally time: the commissioner called out Connor's name, and everyone in the room cheered. Connor Bedard was now a real NHL player! It made his heart beat fast as he hugged his family and shook hands with people from the team. It had been worth all the trouble and hard work.

When Connor was picked, the team knew they were getting more than just a good player. The person they hired had a great attitude, worked hard, and loved the game, which made him stand out. Even with all the attention on him, Connor was able to stay humble and focused. This made him a unique player. He wanted to be more than just the best player on the ice. He also wanted to be the best friend and person he could be.

After being picked up by the team, Connor continued his journey with the same drive that had helped him get this far. He knew that getting into the NHL was just the start. The real work would now start. He was ready to train hard, learn from more experienced players, and work hard to earn a spot on the team. Connor was just as excited about the future as he was determined to do well at the next level.

It wasn't just Connor who felt proud at the NHL draft; everyone who had helped him along the way did too. His coaches, coworkers, family, and friends all helped him reach his goal, and now they could join him in celebrating. The draft wasn't the end of Connor's trip, though. It was the beginning of something even bigger.

I couldn't help but think about all the other kids like him who wanted to play in the NHL one day as he put on his new team's jersey and stood for pictures. He thought that telling them his story would encourage them to work hard, never give up, and always have faith in themselves, just like he had.

For Connor Bedard, getting picked up in the NHL draft was a dream come true. But it was also just the beginning of a long journey. With his skill, hard work, and love for the game, he was ready to take on the task of playing at the highest level. He would continue to make a big difference in the world of hockey.

Fun Facts About Connor Bedard

1. He's the First Player in WHL History to Earn "Exceptional Status"!

At just 15 years old, Connor Bedard became the first player ever to be granted exceptional player status in the Western Hockey League (WHL). This allowed him to play in the league a year early—proving he was already ahead of the game!

2. He's a Goal-Scoring Machine!

Connor has been known to score goals from almost anywhere on the ice. His quick release and accurate shot make him one of the most feared goal scorers in junior hockey. In fact, by his second season in the WHL, Connor was already leading the league in points!

3. He Represented Canada at Just 15 Years Old

At the 2021 IIHF U18 World Championship, Connor helped lead Team Canada to win a gold medal! He was one of the youngest players in the tournament, but that didn't stop him from being one of the best on the ice, scoring important goals for his team.

4. He Loves to Watch Hockey Highlights

Even though Connor is a star player himself, he still loves to learn by watching other great players. He enjoys watching hockey highlight videos in his free time to pick up new moves and study how the best players in the world perform.

5. Connor Was Drafted First Overall!

It didn't come as much of a surprise when Connor was drafted first overall in the WHL Bantam Draft in 2020. Being selected first showed just how highly teams valued his talent, and it set him up to have an amazing career with the Regina Pats.

6. He Was Already Famous at 14

Even before joining the WHL, Connor's talent was so obvious that hockey fans and scouts were already talking about him when he was just 14! Videos of his amazing goals and slick moves went viral, making him one of the most famous young hockey players in the world.

7. He's Known for His Powerful Shot

One of Connor's signature skills is his quick and powerful shot. He has a special ability to fire the puck with incredible accuracy and speed, making it difficult for goalies to stop. His shot is often compared to some of the best shooters in the NHL!

8. He's a Big Fan of the Outdoors

Growing up in British Columbia, Connor spent a lot of time enjoying the outdoors. Whether it was hiking, playing other sports, or just enjoying nature, being active outside helped him become a well-rounded athlete.

9. He Always Works to Improve

Even though he's been called a hockey prodigy, Connor never stops trying to get better. Whether it's practicing his shot, working on his skating, or studying the game, Connor knows that hard work is the key to staying on top of his game.

10. He Inspires Future Hockey Players

Kids all over Canada and the world look up to Connor Bedard as an example of what's possible with hard work, determination, and a love for the game. He shows young athletes that even big dreams can come true with enough effort!

Connor's Message to Young Athletes

"Hey, future athletes! If you've got big dreams, I want you to know that you can make them come true—just like I'm working to do every day. Here are some things I've learned on my hockey journey that might help you, no matter what sport you play!

First, believe in yourself. It all starts with believing you can do great things. When I was younger, I always dreamed of playing in the NHL, and even when things got tough, I held onto that belief. No matter what others say, trust that you can achieve your goals if you put your mind to it.

Work hard and never give up. Nothing worth having comes easy. Whether it's practicing your shots, going to early morning practices, or doing extra drills after school, you've got to be willing to put in the effort. Hard work is what separates good players from great ones, and it's the one thing you can always control.

Stay positive, even when things get tough. There will be times when things don't go your way, whether it's a tough loss, not making a team, or just having a bad day on the ice. But that's okay! What matters most is how you bounce back. Staying positive helps you keep improving and having fun along the way.

Love what you do. The most important thing about playing sports is to enjoy it. I love every moment I spend on the ice, whether it's scoring goals, practicing, or just playing with my teammates. If you have fun and love what you're doing, you'll always want to keep going, no matter how hard it gets.

Learn from others. Watch your teammates, your favorite players, and even your opponents. There's always something new to learn. I spend a lot of time studying how other great players move and shoot, and I try to take something from their game to make mine better. Never stop learning!

Finally, be a good teammate. Sports aren't just about what you can do—they're about how you support your team. Celebrate their successes, lift them when things are tough, and always work together. The best teams are like families, and great teammates make each other better.

So keep working hard, stay positive, and always believe in yourself. You never know where your journey will take you. Just remember—anything is possible if you love what you do and give it your all!"

Hockey Drills Inspired by Connor: Practice Like the Prodigy

Want to train like Connor Bedard? Here are some fun hockey drills that will help you improve your skating, shooting, and puck handling—just like Connor!

---

1. Quick Release Shooting Drill

Connor is known for his lightning-fast shot, and this drill will help you work on getting the puck off your stick quickly and accurately.

What You'll Need: A net and some pucks.

How to Do It:

- Set up a pile of pucks a few feet away from the net.
- Skate toward the puck, and as soon as you reach it, shoot quickly without taking too much time to line up your shot.
- Practice shooting from different angles and distances.

- Focus on getting the shot off fast, just like Connor does in game situations!

Tip: Keep your knees bent and hands ready to release the puck as soon as it's in position.

---

2. Tight Turns and Agility

Connor's speed and ability to change directions quickly are key to his success. This drill will help you improve your agility and control when making quick turns.

What You'll Need: 4 cones (or anything you can use as markers).

How to Do It:

- Set up the cones in a square about 10 feet apart from each other.
- Skate around the cones in a figure-eight pattern, making tight turns at each corner.
- As you get more comfortable, increase your speed and focus on keeping control of the puck while turning.
- Once you're good with the figure-eight, challenge yourself by moving the cones closer together!

Tip: Keep your knees bent and stay low to the ice to make sharp, controlled turns.

---

3. One-Timer Drill

Connor often scores with powerful one-timer shots, which means shooting the puck right after receiving a pass. This drill helps you practice getting that perfect one-timer!

What You'll Need: A net, a stick, a puck, and a partner (or a passer machine if you have one).

How to Do It:

- Stand in front of the net or off to the side, ready to shoot.

- Have your partner pass the puck to you.

- As soon as the puck reaches your stick, take a quick shot without stopping to handle the puck.

- Focus on hitting the puck with accuracy and power as soon as it reaches you.

Tip: Keep your eye on the puck and be ready to adjust your position to get the best shot.

---

4. Puck Control Obstacle Course

Connor's puck-handling skills are second to none, and this drill will help you improve your stick handling while skating.

What You'll Need: 6-8 cones or any objects you can use as obstacles and a puck.

How to Do It:

- Set up the cones in a zigzag pattern a few feet apart.

- Start at one end and stickhandle the puck through the cones as quickly and smoothly as possible.

- Focus on keeping the puck close to your stick while moving around each cone.

- As you get better, try doing the drill faster, or move the cones closer together for a greater challenge.

Tip: Keep your head up as much as possible to simulate game conditions where you need to be aware of your surroundings.

---

5. Skating Sprints with Stops

Connor's speed is one of his greatest strengths, and this drill will help you increase your skating power and endurance.

What You'll Need: A clear patch of ice.

How to Do It:

- Start at one end of the rink and skate as fast as you can to the other end.

- When you reach the far end, stop quickly using a hockey stop, then sprint back to the starting point.

- Repeat this drill for 5-10 sprints, focusing on skating at full speed and making quick, controlled stops.

Tip: Keep your knees bent and pump your arms to help drive your legs forward as you sprint.

---

6. Stickhandling in Tight Spaces

Connor often faces opponents up close and needs to keep control of the puck in small spaces. This drill helps you work on your puck control in tight areas.

What You'll Need: 4-6 cones (or obstacles), and a puck.

How to Do It:

- Set up the cones close together in a small area.
- Stickhandle the puck through the cones as tightly as you can, focusing on keeping the puck under control.
- Try to move the puck in all directions—left, right, forward, and backward—while keeping it close to your stick.

Tip: Soft hands are key—focus on gently moving the puck and keeping it within reach at all times.

---

7. Backhand Shot Practice

Connor is a master at scoring from all angles, including using his backhand shot. This drill will help you improve your backhand shot, which can be tricky but very effective!

What You'll Need: A net and a pile of pucks.

How to Do It:

- Stand a few feet away from the net with the pucks lined up.

- Practice lifting the puck into the net using only your backhand.

- Start close to the net, then slowly move farther back as you get more comfortable.

- Work on getting height and accuracy with each backhand shot.

Tip: Focus on the motion of your wrists and follow through to generate power on your backhand.

These drills will help you practice the skills that make Connor Bedard one of the best young players in hockey. Remember, just like Connor, consistency and hard work are the keys to improving, so keep practicing and have fun on the ice!

Q&A: Test Your Knowledge

Let's see how much you know about Connor Bedard! Answer these simple questions to test your hockey knowledge.

---

1. How old was Connor when he started playing in the WHL?

A) 12 years old

B) 15 years old

C) 18 years old

D) 20 years old

---

2. What sport does Connor Bedard play?

A) Basketball

B) Soccer

C) Hockey

D) Tennis

---

3. What is Connor Bedard good at?

A) Running fast

B) Playing the drums

C) Shooting the puck quickly and scoring goals

D) Cooking

---

4. Which country is Connor Bedard from?

A) United States

B) Canada

C) Australia

D) England

---

5. What's the name of the league where Connor played as a teenager?

A) NHL

B) WHL

C) NBA

D) MLB

---

6. What is Connor's position in hockey?

A) Goalie

B) Forward (Center)

C) Referee

D) Cheerleader

---

7. What does Connor like to do in his free time?

A) Watch hockey videos

B) Ride horses

C) Play the piano

D) Paint

---

8. What does Connor Bedard believe in to get better at hockey?

A) Playing video games

B) Taking naps

C) Working hard and practicing

D) Skipping practice

---

9. What team did Connor play for in the WHL?

A) Calgary Hitmen

B) Regina Pats

C) Edmonton Oil Kings

D) Vancouver Canucks

---

10. What country has Connor played for in international tournaments?

A) Canada

B) Spain

C) Japan

D) Italy

How did you do? If you got all the answers right, you know a lot about Connor Bedard!

Conclusion

Connor Bedard's story is one of passion, hard work, and determination. From the moment he first stepped onto the ice as a young boy in British Columbia, it was clear that he had something special. But more than just his natural talent, it was Connor's dedication to getting better every single day that has set him apart. His journey from playing on local rinks to becoming one of the most exciting young hockey players in the world is a story that shows how far hard work can take you.

Becoming the first player in WHL history to earn "exceptional status" was only the beginning of Connor's rise. He wasn't afraid to face challenges, whether it was playing against older, more experienced players or stepping onto the international stage to represent Canada. Every time he faced a new challenge, Connor met it head-on, always looking for ways to improve. His ability to stay focused, work hard, and keep a positive attitude is what makes him a true role model, not just for young hockey players, but for anyone with big dreams.

What's amazing about Connor's journey is that it's a reminder that success doesn't come overnight. It takes years of practice, commitment, and never giving up. Connor didn't just wake up one day as a hockey star—he spent hours and hours on the ice, shooting pucks, improving his skating, and learning from others. Even when things didn't go his way, he kept going, knowing that every setback was just another chance to get better. His dedication to his craft has shown young athletes everywhere that if you want to be great, you have to put in the effort.

But it's not just about the hard work—Connor also teaches us the importance of loving what you do. He plays hockey with joy and passion, always having fun, even during tough practices or big games. His love for the sport keeps him motivated and excited to keep improving. It's this passion that has helped him stay grounded, no matter how much success he's found at a young age. And it's a reminder to all of us that when you love what you do, the hard work doesn't feel like a burden—it feels like a part of the journey.

Another important lesson from Connor's story is the value of believing in yourself. From the time he was a little kid dreaming of playing in the NHL, Connor never stopped believing that he could achieve his goals. Even when others doubted him, or when the road got tough, he kept believing that if he put in the work, he could reach his dreams. His confidence and belief in himself have been key to his success, and it's a powerful reminder for anyone chasing big goals—you have to trust in your abilities and stay focused on the path ahead.

Connor's journey also highlights the importance of being a good teammate and supporting others. Hockey is a team sport, and while Connor's talent stands out, he always works hard to help his teammates succeed. He's the kind of player who celebrates not just his own goals, but the success of his team. Connor understands that being a great player also means being a great teammate—lifting others, working together, and striving for success as a group.

Now, as Connor continues to rise in the hockey world, his story is far from over. The future holds incredible things for him, and there's no doubt that we'll continue to see him break records, score amazing goals, and inspire others with his talent and hard work. But more importantly, his journey reminds us that anyone with a big dream can achieve great things if they work hard, stay focused, and never give up.

So, what can we all learn from Connor Bedard? No matter what your dream is—whether it's in sports, school, or something else—always believe in yourself, work as hard as you can, and enjoy the process. There will be tough moments along the way, but those are the times when you grow stronger. And like Connor, if you stay positive and keep going, you'll get closer to your goals every day.

As Connor Bedard's journey continues, he'll keep inspiring young athletes all around the world, showing them that greatness isn't just about talent—it's about heart, effort, and passion for what you do. So, if you have a dream, remember: to keep working, stay humble, and always believe that you can make it. Just like Connor Bedard, you too can achieve amazing things!

Made in the USA
Columbia, SC
23 December 2024